Written and illustrated

by Sophie Marvell.

There are lots of wild creatures living in Britain, even if you can't always see them. They're all very excited to introduce themselves to you...

I am the hedgehog.

I am a nocturnal animal, which means I sleep during the day and I am awake at night, except when I snuggle up and sleep through all of winter. This is called hibernation.

During the night, whilst you are sleeping, I feast on lots of tasty grubs. My favourites are worms, beetles and slugs.

I am the roe deer.

In the winter my coat is brown and thick, perfect for keeping me warm and cosy.

In the summer my coat turns a beautiful orange and is much thinner, so I stay cooler.

I am the honey bee.

My job is to pass pollen from flower to flower, so they can grow. This is called pollination and is very important for keeping all the plants alive.

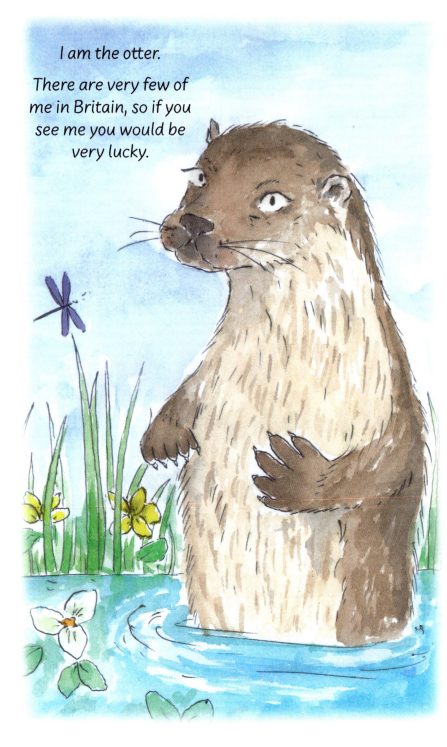

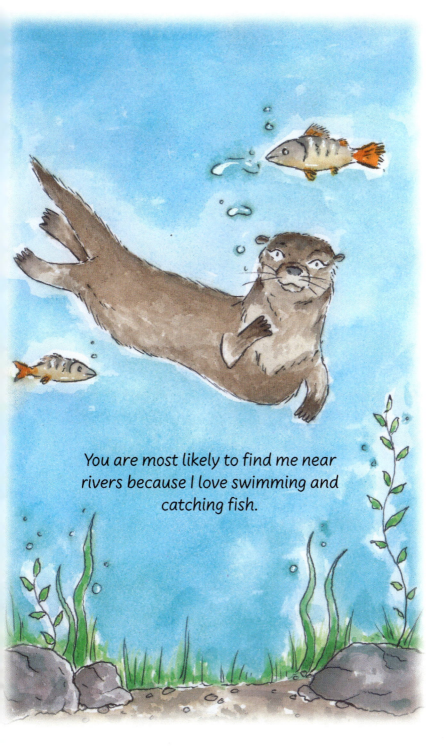

I am the grey squirrel.

In the warmer months I collect lots of nuts and seeds and bury them ready for winter, when food is sparse.

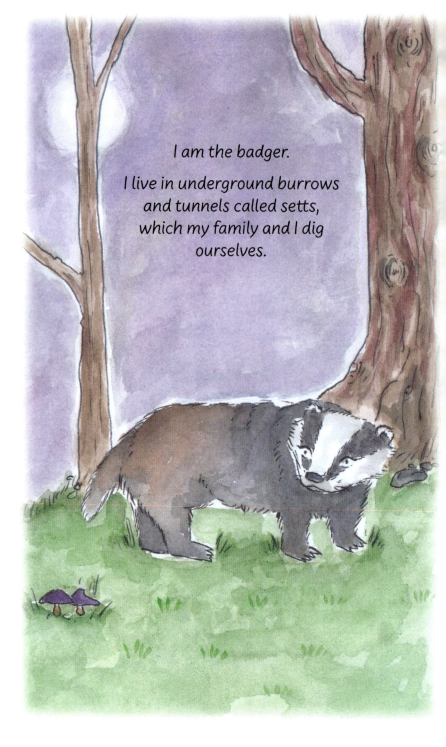

I am the badger.

I live in underground burrows and tunnels called setts, which my family and I dig ourselves.

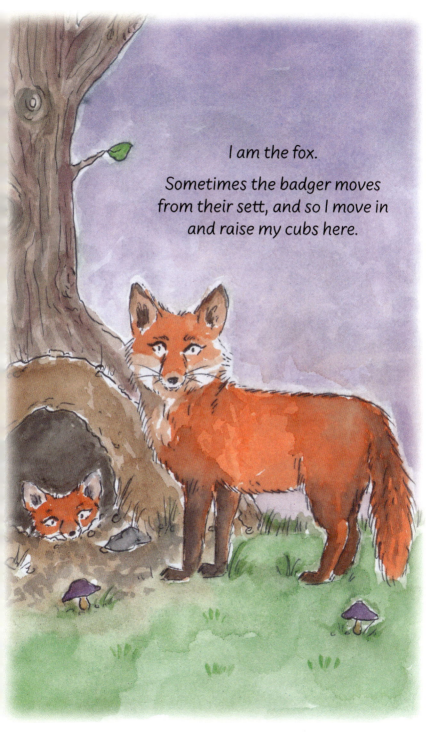

I am the common frog.

I am an amphibian which means I can live in and out of water.

You can also hear me pecking away in the treetops. I will be making a nest so I can raise my young.

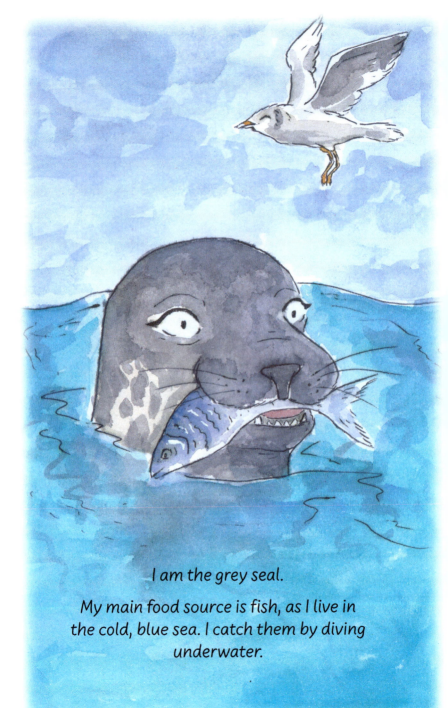

I am the grey seal.

My main food source is fish, as I live in the cold, blue sea. I catch them by diving underwater.

To digest my food, I come out of the water and rest on the shore. This is called 'hauling out'.

I am the harvest mouse.

I am much smaller than a normal mouse. I mainly live in cornfields and build my nest above the ground, around the stalks of plants.

Printed in Great Britain
by Amazon